EXECUTIVE COACHING

AN ANNOTATED BIBLIOGRAPHY

EXECUTIVE COACHING

AN ANNOTATED BIBLIOGRAPHY

Christina A. Douglas
William H. Morley

Center for Creative Leadership
Greensboro, North Carolina

The Center for Creative Leadership is an international, nonprofit educational institution founded in 1970 to advance the understanding, practice, and development of leadership for the benefit of society worldwide. As a part of this mission, it publishes books and reports that aim to contribute to a general process of inquiry and understanding in which ideas related to leadership are raised, exchanged, and evaluated. The ideas presented in its publications are those of the author or authors.

The Center thanks you for supporting its work through the purchase of this volume. If you have comments, suggestions, or questions about any Center publication, please contact John R. Alexander, President, at the address given below.

Center for Creative Leadership
Post Office Box 26300
Greensboro, North Carolina 27438-6300

Center for
Creative Leadership

leadership. learning. life.

©2000 Center for Creative Leadership
Reprinted January 2001

CCL No. 347

Library of Congress Cataloging-in-Publication Data

Douglas, Christina A.
   Executive coaching : an annotated bibliography / Christina A. Douglas, William H. Morley
     p. cm.
   Includes bibliographical references and indexes.
   ISBN 1-882197-55-0
   1. Management—Study and teaching—Bibliography. 2. Executives—Training of—Bibliography. 3. Mentoring in business—Bibliography. 4. Business consultants—Bibliography. I. Morley, William H. II. Title.

Z7164.O7 D68 2000
[HD30.4]
016.6584'07124—dc21
                                            00-027958

Table of Contents

Preface

For the past several years researchers at the Center for Creative Leadership (CCL) have been studying the role of developmental relationships. This stream of research has fostered an increasing interest in executive coaching and its impact on the leadership development process. In addition to developing a research strategy around executive coaching, CCL provides an executive coaching program as a follow-up to some of its existing leadership development programs.

This book joins those efforts as a review of the professional literature that focuses on executive coaching. We are grateful to the writers and researchers behind that body of literature, and to CCL for publishing this book as a means of disseminating important knowledge about the field of executive coaching.

We also thank several specific individuals who helped us with this book. Patti Hall, Debbie Nelson, and Carole Sumner assisted us in identifying and obtaining references. Marcia Horowitz and Pete Scisco provided helpful editorial guidance and support through the book's development and subsequent drafts, and Joanne Ferguson guided the book's final layout and production.

For their roles as reviewers, we owe thanks to Larry Osborne, professor of counseling and educational development at the University of North Carolina at Greensboro and adjunct program associate at CCL; Karen Kirkland Miller, feedback and coaching manager at CCL; and Amy Webb, CCL adjunct faculty member and principal of The Webb Group in Greensboro, for their valuable suggestions for improving this book.

Introduction

Organizations recognize with increasing frequency the value of on-the-job developmental relationships as important sources of managerial learning and career development. These relationships can be informal or formal and can take various forms, including one-on-one mentoring, peer coaching, team coaching, and executive coaching.

As one type of formal developmental relationship, executive coaching can be defined as a short-term relationship between an executive and a consultant (from inside or outside the organization) that is created to achieve specific, mutually agreed-upon performance goals.

The past several years have brought an explosion of interest in executive coaching in terms of the number of practicing executive coaches in the United States and in the number of individuals and organizations seeking out executive-coaching relationships and establishing executive-coaching initiatives. This rise in demand has been met by a rise in the amount of published work focusing on executive coaching. The purpose of this book is to summarize this growing body of literature by annotating books and articles that pertain specifically to executive coaching.

The book is divided into two sections. The first section contains annotations to 49 works, which are representative of the available published literature on executive coaching. The annotations are descriptive summaries intended to help readers decide whether or not the complete work has bearing on their work with executive coaching.

The book's second section organizes and describes some of the broad implications and issues that the annotated sources bring to light. It addresses definitions of executive coaching, descriptions of the coaching process, a discussion of executive coaching goals, a look at the impact of executive coaching, and a discussion of the implications and future needs of executive coaching.

The articles and books that are annotated in this report were chosen by doing a thorough search of the available current literature on the subject, including both academic and practitioner-oriented sources. Two databases were searched: *Psych-Lit* and *ABI-Inform*. We grant that these sources are not exhaustive, but we believe them to be highly representative of current thinking on the topic of executive coaching. We narrowed our search to published articles appearing in the past ten years that centered specifically on executive coaching. We further narrowed our selections by excluding articles that repeated material presented in another article (for example, two articles by the same author that contained the same content) and that did not add substance to the existing literature (for example, articles that were poorly written, contained very little content, or voiced opinions irrelevant to the field). In general, we found fewer articles than we had expected, and so excluded articles only if they were obviously poor in content or had very little to say about executive coaching.

This book is intended primarily for those who want to learn more about executive coaching, including executives looking for coaching possibilities, human resources professionals charged with creating a coaching initiative, and coaches themselves. Secondarily, the executive's boss, his or her co-workers, and even family members may find the annotations collected here useful to their understanding of the coaching process. Researchers needing access to this literature for their own work can also find value in this book.

Annotated Bibliography

Altier, W. J. (1989, October). The executive coach. *Executive Excellence,*
   6(10), 11-12.

   The author, a management consultant, argued that before executives can
coach others, they may need to be coached by a special breed of management
consultant who can help them coach their associates toward superior performance. Altier made comparisons between the athletic coach and the management coach, between the employer and fans, and between stockholders and
the marketplace. Further, he claimed that the role of the executive coach is to
assist the executive in acquiring distance and objectivity in order to solve
problems.

   Altier listed several purposes of the executive coach role: to act as an
executive's sounding board, catalyst, facilitator, and productivity booster; to
help executives "improve their edge"; to help executives better organize their
thinking and to see things from a broader, more complete perspective; to help
executives see concerns more objectively; to lead executives into exercising
their creative powers in developing problem-solving options that might
otherwise be overlooked; and to help executives understand their relative
position and significance in a given situation. After working with a coach
who fulfills these purposes, the author said, an executive can reduce uncertainty and can expect to have greater confidence.

***

Beckhard, R. (1997). *Agent of change: My life, my practice*. San Francisco:
   Jossey-Bass, 304 pages.

   In this autobiographical account of his life and career, Beckhard focused on his work as an organization development consultant. In addition to
his account of serving as an executive coach, the author also provided advice
to coaches and would-be coaches. He stressed the importance of realizing that
the client, not the coach, owns the specific problem being addressed. It is the
coach's job to help, not to control.

   Using sports coaching as a metaphor, Beckhard emphasized that an
executive coach provides an educational intervention that allows the client to
develop more capacity to manage change and development. The relationship
should be kept professional and periodic, and the client should be encouraged
to engage in dreaming, visioning, and creative thinking. Clients should be
encouraged and rewarded for making progress in their competence and
confidence. The coach should provide informal and formal feedback on the
effectiveness of the client's actions.

***

Benton, D. A. (1999). *Secrets of a CEO coach: Your personal training guide to thinking like a leader and acting like a CEO.* New York: McGraw-Hill, 211 pages.

Benton is president of her own research and consulting firm specializing in executive coaching and development. Her book was written for executives who want to coach themselves and for executive coaching professionals who want to more clearly understand the issues facing corporate executives. The book covered such topics as defining a business coach, knowing when one is needed, selecting the right coach, coaching others, and CEO techniques that can be applied to daily management practices.

This annotation focuses on two chapters: "What Is a Business Coach?" and "Team Time: How to Coach Others."

In "What Is a Business Coach?" Benton defined the business coach as someone who "works with you privately to provide objective, professional direction to increase your performance by helping you enhance what you have and acquire what you need." The coach assists the executive in recognizing behaviors that hinder effectiveness in leading and managing. The author suggested that good coaches are professionally qualified, objective, and motivational. They can establish rapport with a wide variety of people, can ask the right questions, can assess and keep track of effective and problem behaviors, can criticize constructively while providing positive encouragement, and can care for the client's self-esteem. They can also act as a colleague, not as a competitor.

In this chapter Benton also described what happens during a coaching session and the process for coaching a client over a period of time. She described a few reasons why executives often seek coaching: improving personal and professional presence, dealing effectively with difficult people, working with people whom the executive perceives as not very smart, and being more personable.

In the chapter "Team Time: How to Coach Others," Benton discussed how the coached executive can act as a coach to others and offered ten rules for effective coaching: (1) cultivate the attitude that you have something of value to offer, (2) be an impeccable example, (3) shelve your ego, (4) slow down to appear more self-assured and to gain more time to think, (5) constantly raise the bar for yourself and learn from experience, (6) hold your ground and do not be intimidated by the client, (7) give superlative advice but do not be bothered if the client doesn't apply it, (8) admit mistakes, (9) be willing to extricate the client from unfortunate situations your advice might have created, and (10) stay impartial.

***

Brotherton, P. R. (1998, June). Making a connection: It's time for a career workout. *Black Enterprise*, *28*(11), 82.

Aimed at individuals who might be interested in hiring a career coach, this article briefly described executive coaching and presented two case studies. The author differentiated between coaches and management consultants by defining coaches as using a personalized, philosophical approach that focuses on career and life issues and ensuring progress by following up with clients, rather than presenting one-shot solutions to specific management problems. According to the article, coaching sessions are typically about thirty minutes long, held on a weekly or monthly basis, and cost $300 to $1,500 depending on the coach and the complexity of the issues. The typical client is a successful professional in some type of career transition.

The author made four recommendations for individuals looking for a good executive coach: get personal referrals, interview at least three coaches, evaluate potential coaches' credentials and experience, and seek out a compatible style.

***

Brotman, L. E., Liberi, W. P., & Wasylyshyn, K. M. (1998). Executive coaching: The need for standards of competence. *Consulting Psychology Journal: Practice and Research*, *50*(1), 40-46.

These management consultants and psychologists saw a strong need for educating corporate decision-makers on the core skills, competencies, experiences, and related professional issues needed to forge successful outcomes in executive coaching. They cautioned the reader that executive coaching is an unregulated and poorly defined professional category. Because there are no licenses, credentials, or professional designations in this field, the client should set guidelines to identify competent, ethical executive coaches.

The authors identified twelve competencies for the effective executive coach: approachability, self-knowledge, comfort around top management, intellectual horsepower, compassion, interpersonal savvy, creativity, listening, customer focus, political savvy, integrity and trust, and the ability to deal with paradox.

In addition to possessing these competencies, the effective executive coach must have a background or have experience in the field of psychology in order to sustain behavioral change in a client. That grounding enables

coaches to identify behavior patterns in clients that erode leadership effectiveness, to convert insights into behavior change, and to be absolutely honest in
appraising the client's behavior in relation to the organization and the situation. What the authors called the "Triple T Proficiency Model" for executive
coaching (tactics, tools, and training) would, they argued, help provide
authority to the practice of executive coaching.

∗∗∗

Diedrich, R. C. (1996). An iterative approach to executive coaching. *Consulting Psychology Journal*: *Practice and Research, 48*(2), 61-66.

A senior consultant who specializes in executive assessment and development, Diedrich offered in this article a case-study approach to executive
coaching. He views his executive coach role as a value-added activity designed to help the executive focus on issues such as identifying and modifying the impact of managerial style on individuals and/or teams, adapting to
change, using key strengths, planning and monitoring developmental
progress, enhancing organizational performance, and learning the key dimensions of executive performance.

Deidrich specified three key elements to his executive coaching style:
(1) develop and maintain an interactive learning process that focuses on
developing the client's awareness and insight regarding planning and implementing choices or alternative behaviors for better executive performance;
(2) deal with the executive holistically in making feedback a two-way process
that is specific, empathetic, engaged, responsive, and directed toward desired
outcomes; and (3) ensure that the executive and the organization view the
coaching process as an ongoing activity and developmental process for
executive growth, not a quick fix.

The author concluded with a case study involving a plant manager in
his mid-forties. He described the various data-gathering processes, one-to-one
coaching sessions, action steps, and evaluation that client experienced.
Additionally, Deidrich continued the theme of a holistic approach to effective
executive coaching by noting the intersection of the coaching relationship
with the client's boss and organization.

∗∗∗

Douglas, C. A., & McCauley, C. D. (1997). A survey on the use of formal
developmental relationships in organizations. *Issues & Observations,
17*(1/2), 6-9.

This article described a study in which a random sample of 246 U.S.
corporations were interviewed to examine their use of formal developmental

relationships (defined as any formal initiative that pairs employees with peers, senior managers, or outside consultants for the purposes of learning and development) as a management-development strategy. Based on an 82% response rate, findings were obtained regarding the frequency of such pairings, expectations regarding future use of developmental relationships, program characteristics, program visibility, and program effectiveness. Fifty-two of the organizations indicated that they had at least one such program in place. Sixty programs were reported and described.

Types of formal relationships reported included one-on-one mentoring, apprenticeships, peer coaching, action learning, team coaching, and executive coaching. Only four organizations reported the use of executive coaching programs. The reported purpose of these four programs was to help senior managers who had been identified as needing improvement in particular skill areas (interpersonal skills, for example). As a rule the managers were paired with external coaches who worked with them for relatively short periods of time (typically about six months). These relationships tended to be highly confidential within the organization and were open-ended (executive coaches were brought in when needed). Because of the confidential nature of many executive coaching programs, the authors argued it was reasonable to assume that the frequency and level of executive coaching taking place within organizations is higher than was reported by this survey.

* * *

Dutton, G. (1997). Executive coaches call the plays. *Management Review, 86(2)*, 39-43.

The author is a business writer whose article presented a holistic approach to executive coaching that takes into account life-balance issues, family history, a personal profile of goals and objectives, and insight into how to be more effective in business.

Dutton raised six key questions that executives should ask when deciding whether to hire a coach: (1) Are you willing to think beyond what you currently believe and assume? (2) Are you committed to operating at the leading edge? (3) Are you willing to restructure your life? (4) Do you recognize that people are one's most valuable asset? (5) Are you committed to being a visionary leader? (6) Do you need to maintain a high level of accomplishment?

* * *

Foster, S., & Lendl, J. (1996). Eye movement desensitization and reprocessing: Four case studies of a new tool for executive coaching and restoring
  employee performance after setbacks. *Consulting Psychology Journal:*
  Practice and Research, 48(3), 155-161.

     This study reported the findings from four case studies of executive
coaching that incorporated a technique called "eye movement desensitization
and reprocessing" (EMDR). The participants included a pilot, a university
professor, a former CEO, and an office manager. Three of these participants
had experienced perceived setbacks that had impaired their productivity,
while the last participant (the university professor) was seeking a career
change and desired assistance with her performance anxiety about interviewing. As a part of the EMDR coaching process, the participants were asked to
describe the upsetting situation and describe their negative beliefs about
themselves. The participants were then encouraged to initiate a cognitive
restructuring process whereby they were asked to think about the incident in
terms of a positive belief about themselves. After this cognitive restructuring,
each participant was asked to follow the coach's fingers with his or her eyes
in order to produce between 12 and 24 multidirectional eye movements. Each
participant was asked to think about the distressing incident again and repeat
the eye movements until the distressing incident was desensitized and the
negative belief was fully reconstructed as a positive belief. The findings
indicated that the EMDR process appeared to desensitize the disturbing
incident and that participants shifted their negative view to a more positive
one. Further, the article suggested that EMDR may have potential as an
adjunct to coaching for workplace performance enhancement.

                                    * * *

Filipczak, B. (1998). The executive coach: Helper or healer? *Training, 35*(3),
  30-36.

     Using case examples and discussions with executive coaches, research-
ers, and clients, the author discussed the current thinking about the various
roles of executive coaches. While some executive coaches focus on helping
senior executives think through their company's strategic direction, other
coaches act as agents who look out for the individual interests of their clients.
Still others adopt a broader view and approach coaching as a type of therapy.

     According to the article, the majority of executive coaches are hired to
help executives improve their interpersonal skills as opposed to their business
skills. The rapid increase in the amount of executive coaching that is taking
place can be attributed to several factors. For example, it was argued that not

only does a corporate leadership position demand much more complicated interpersonal skills than in past years, but also managers receive more and better assessments of their interpersonal skills than did their predecessors. For managers at the top of an organization, a lack of informal feedback is common; often the most valuable part of the executive coach's relationship with a client is the role of a sounding board.

***

Gould, D. (1997). Developing directors through personal coaching. *Long Range Planning, 30*(1), 29-37.

As a coaching consultant for many years, this author used observation, debate, and practical application in his approach to developing directors. According to this article, directing is distinct from management. Without fully defining management, the author established that while managers control processes and implement policy, directors carry the legal burdens, are involved in setting strategy and policy, and are responsible for corporate governance.

Helping directors identify how they need to develop involves deciding which organizational processes are ineffective and inventing more up-to-date methods. The author argued for a six-stage course, which included induction, inclusion, competence, performance, plateau, and transition, and illustrated these stages with a case study.

Because both the organization and the individual directors are different in each situation, the author said coaching programs must be adjusted to fit specific needs. Coaching efforts should start at the top of a business, so that the process is legitimized for all employees and so directors can send strong messages throughout the organization.

The author used three examples to illustrate various coaching strategies. All showed that the individual's processes must parallel the corporate processes and that where there is neither personal nor organizational development the corporate strategy is not achieved.

***

Guthrie, V. A. (1999). *Coaching for action: A report on long-term advising in a program context*. Greensboro, NC: Center for Creative Leadership, 56 pages.

This report documented the creation, implementation, and evaluation of what the Center for Creative Leadership (CCL) calls a *process advisor*. Within the context of LeaderLab®, a leadership development program designed and offered by CCL, the process advisor plays a coaching-and-support role and works closely with program participants for anywhere from six months to a year.

The report concluded with a short developmental relationship assessment exercise, focusing on the types and intent of various coaching roles.

* * *

Hall, D. T., Otazo, K. L., & Hollenbeck, G. P. (1999). Behind the closed doors: What really happens in executive coaching. *Organizational Dynamics, 27*(3), 39-53.

This article described executive coaching in terms of definitions, practices, processes, outcomes, and controversies. The authors base their insights on a research study consisting of interviews with over 75 executives who have participated in executive coaching and with 15 executive coaches.

The authors contrasted and compared internal executive coaches (typically a human resources staff person) and external executive coaches. Advantages of using an external coach include anonymity, confidentiality, the coach's business experience, expertise, and objectivity. Advantages of an internal coach included knowledge of organizational politics and culture, easy availability, personal trust (the opportunity for the executive to develop a high degree of personal trust toward the coach over a long period of time), and the ability to help in identifying highest priorities.

Because internal coaches can serve a dual role, with accountability to both the organization and to the executive, a potential conflict of interest may arise as an issue. External coaches, by contrast, have a less ambivalent relationship with the executive.

The authors also attempted to identify what comprises effective executive coaching. Executives interviewed cited honest, reliable feedback and good action ideas as the two primary factors of effective coaching. Other characteristics of effective coaching included good listening, objectivity, lack of personal agenda, accessibility, and competence. The executive coaches interviewed listed effective coaching elements such as maintaining a personal connection with the client, good listening, reflecting, caring, demonstrating a trial-and-error attitude toward learning, following up, commitment to client success, integrity, openness, and pushing the client when necessary. Neither executives nor coaches cited gender as a significant component to the coaching relationship.

Most of the clients interviewed said they were very satisfied with their coaching experience and felt that the coaching process led to their acquiring new skills, abilities, and perspectives. From this information, the authors cited

four types of learning or coaching outcomes: task performance and effectiveness, change in personal attitude and perspective (more patience and improved confidence, for example), adaptability, and identity change.

Although confident about the potential impact and success of executive
coaching, the authors cited three major concerns about the future of executive
coaching. First, managing the growing demand for executive coaching will be
a difficult challenge facing organizations. Second, it is necessary for companies to address the important ethical issues arising from the use of coaches,
especially internal coaches. Finally, as the scale and scope of executive
coaching grows, it is important that organizations establish clear guidelines
for the use of coaches and for the coaching process, and make executive
coaching a part of the organization's development opportunities.

***

Hamilton, K. (1996, February 5). Need a life? Get a coach. *Newsweek*,
    127(6), 48.

With examples and brief case studies, this article highlighted the
growing use of executive coaching by managers and entrepreneurs. Executive
coaches help individuals define and achieve professional and personal goals.
They play such roles as consultant, motivational speaker, therapist, and rent-
a-friend. A typical coaching relationship might involve weekly half-hour
sessions for a six-month period for fees ranging from $150 to $500 a month.
Proponents of executive coaching believe that the field will undergo tremen-
dous growth within the next five years. Coaches are still not subject to regula-
tion or licensing requirements, and there are no current industry standards on
appropriate counseling processes.

***

Hargrove, R. (1995). *Masterful coaching: Extraordinary results by impacting
    people and the way they think and work together.* San Francisco: Pfeiffer/
    Jossey-Bass, 320 pages.

Robert Hargrove is the founder of Hargrove & Partners and Transformational Learning Incorporated, a consulting and training services firm. This
three-part book reflected the author's theme of "transformational coaching,"
which he defined as "unleashing the human spirit and helping people learn
powerful lessons in personal change as well as expand their capacity for
action." Specifically, the book expanded on the author's idea of the "masterful coach." He described such an individual as having the "dream, aspiration,
and the bone-deep commitment to make a difference in the lives of individu-

als, groups, or entire organizations . . . a commitment that unlocks your wisdom, intuition, and insight when mere technique fails."

Part 1, Personal Transformation, dealt with how a coach challenges and supports clients. Hargrove's steps for achieving coaching mastery in this area included mapping the territory, which means the masterful coach enters into the relationship with the intent of improving the client's performance; personal transformation and reinvention, which means the masterful coach empowers clients to create a future they truly desire by expanding the horizon of possibilities, eliciting powerful new commitments, transforming their view of themselves, fostering new ways of being and acting, and helping clients move past obstacles; creating communities of commitment and team collaboration, in which the masterful coach engages the executive in assisting the organization or team in forming a shared vision and purpose; and expanding people's capacity to take effective action, which means the masterful coach helps the executive to take successful actions and to honestly acknowledge when plans go awry. Hargrove ended Part I with a six-point list of the masterful coach's characteristics: the ability to inspire; setting higher standards; honesty and integrity; disciplined intensity; forwarding action; and a passion to help others learn, grow, and perform.

Part II, Coaching for Team Learning: The Fundamentals, moved from one-on-one coaching to coaching a group. The author proposed seven "navigation" points for coaching in a group setting: (1) set stretch goals; (2) elicit internal commitment, motivation, and self-directed learning among team members; (3) create a successful story of action for the group; (4) practice fundamental coaching; (5) observe breakdowns among individuals and in the group as a whole; (6) provide meaningful feedback to individuals and the team; and (7) teach new skills and capabilities.

The book's third part, The Secrets of Masterful Coaching, provided tools, ideas, and methods that can be used by an executive coach. The author explained ideas like "breakthrough thinking," which incorporates the learning process into the coaching process, and "building shared understanding," which teaches executives how to think and interact better as a work group through "collaborative conversations." Other coaching strategies include helping the executive recognize and deal with defensiveness within his or her organization and showing executives how to bring added value to organizations not just by doing new things but also by unlearning old practices.

Hargrove's book balanced theories and real examples to show how executive coaches can build effective strategies and approaches in their practices.

***

Hayes, G. E. (1997). Executive coaching: A strategy for management and organization development. In A. J. Pickman (Ed.), *Special challenges in career management: Counselor perspectives* (pp. 213-222). Mahwah, NJ: Lawrence Erlbaum Associates, 264 pages.

This book chapter outlined the characteristics of effective executive coaches, described who might benefit from executive coaching, and explained the steps in a typical coaching process. An effective coach, according to the author, combines an understanding of human motivation, emotions, and interpersonal styles with an understanding of organizational life. Psychologists and other mental health professionals can be effective in this role if they have a certain level of organizational experience and insight.

Any executive facing new challenges, such as new job responsibilities, can benefit from executive coaching. This process can also benefit executives who need to improve their people-management skills and managerial teams that want to improve their effectiveness.

The author's list of steps found in the typical coaching process are the referral meeting, the initial meeting with the potential client, the assessment session, setting the developmental agenda, and follow-up counseling sessions.

The author also suggested that executive coaching has implications for organizational development, and that it can be employed throughout an entire management level at once. This kind of intervention is useful when the organization has experienced rapid growth because of a high level of technical competence among its professional staff. Executive coaching can help those individuals make the transition from project management to people management.

***

Judge, W. Q., & Cowell, J. (1997). The brave new world of executive coaching. *Business Horizons, 40*(4), 71-77.

Executive coaching, as an outgrowth of executive development programs, is the latest developmental approach to improving the performance of executives, according to this article. Executive coaching practices date back to the early 1980s, but widespread adoption of executive coaching practices began around 1990. The authors defined executive coaching as "a series of one-on-one interactions between a coach and an executive that attempts to improve the latter's performance" (p. 71). Unlike mentors, executive coaches almost always come from outside the organization. Executive coaching has traditionally addressed a performance problem but is also now used to enhance the performance of high-potential managers.

The article presented the findings from a 1996 survey of executive coaches. Only the results were included, without details about the study sample or methodology. The authors did report some interesting findings regarding the characteristics of executive coaches. Approximately 90% have at least master's degrees and about 45% have doctorates; about 60% of the executive coaches surveyed were male; and about 80% of the coaches were between 35 and 55 years old. In approximately one-half of the cases, the executive coaching process was initiated by the executive needing the coaching and in the other half the process was initiated by the executive's supervisor. The typical participant was a mid-level to senior-level executive.

In terms of executive coaching practices, 64% of the executive coaches worked within an independent or small group practice, 29% worked within a large group practice, and 7% were company employees.

The authors identified three broad categories of executives who participate in executive coaching and described the typical coaching process for each of these three categories. The first category included individuals with performance obstacles that prevented advancement. For these participants, coaching typically involved an assessment followed by weekly or biweekly sessions that covered goal setting, taking action, feedback, and follow-up.

The second category of participants included high-potential executives without specific deficiencies but with a desire to improve leadership skills. For this group, coaching typically involved a thorough assessment of strengths and weaknesses and monthly sessions over a period of six to eighteen months.

A third category of participants included professionals and entrepreneurs seeking help with developing long-term strategies for professional and personal growth.

The results of the survey revealed that executive coaching typically focuses on twelve skills. Arranged from most frequent to least frequent in occurrence, they are: modifying interaction style, building trust in relationships, dealing better with change, improving listening skills, improving public speaking, balancing work and personal life, clarifying and pursuing goals, strengthening delegation skills, improving technical skills, handling stress better, improving writing skills, and maintaining a long-term focus.

The authors drew distinctions between executive coaching and traditional psychotherapy. First, coaching is typically a short-term solution with a predefined duration. Executive coaching takes a more holistic approach to the development process by involving individuals other than the client (for, example, supervisors, human resource managers, peers, direct reports, spouses). Executive coaching is typically focused on a particular management area, whereas psychotherapy is less content-specific.

According to the authors, it is important that organizations understand that coaching is aimed at changing behaviors that limit effectiveness and is not effective at changing personality or basic individual values. This understanding is crucial when determining whether a particular individual is a good candidate for executive coaching. In addition, the potential participant must be willing to accept coaching and be able to accurately assess the environment in which the process occurs, accurately judge his or her personal behavior, and be sensitive to the reaction of others. A supportive organizational structure and culture that supports the changes that the participant is trying to make is essential to the success of an executive coaching initiative.

***

Kaplan, R., & Palus, C. J. (1994). *Enhancing 360-degree feedback for senior executives: How to maximize the benefits and minimize the risks.* Greensboro, NC: Center for Creative Leadership, 30 pages.

This report described a type of feedback called *enhanced 360-degree feedback* or *enhanced feedback*. Enhanced feedback adds some or all of the following to standard 360-degree feedback: detailed verbatim descriptions, observations from family members and friends, psychometric measures of personality and motivation, historical data (including family history), and an extended coaching relationship with one or more leadership development professionals.

Although traditional 360-degree feedback is an effective development tool for all management levels, senior managers may sometimes require a richer feedback experience. Compared to other types of managers and executives, senior managers typically face a broader range of challenges. The psychological make-up of individuals who rise to high-level positions (achievement-oriented, forceful, and highly demanding) often undermines their long-term performance. Enhanced 360-degree feedback can provide a powerful tool for addressing performance at the psychological level.

Based on several studies that examine the impact of enhanced feedback and on their experience working with participants, the authors concluded that enhanced feedback is a powerful tool for convincing participants to make the changes needed to develop better performance and leadership skills. The authors also emphasized that negative outcomes are possible, and emphasized safeguards designed to reduce uncertainty for participants. First, only mature staff competent in management development, proficient at personal development, and effective with senior managers should give the enhanced feedback. Second, participants must be carefully selected. Managers who are fragile and who are highly defensive and rigid are not good candidates for enhanced feedback. Finally, participants should have access to support and follow-up that prepares the executive for the feedback, stresses the positive and deals with negative feedback outcomes, refrains from coercing or attacking the executive, stays in touch after the feedback session, and helps the participant gain conceptual and emotional closure on the experience by challenging the executive to make real progress.

* * *

Katz, J. H., & Miller, F. A. (1996). Coaching leaders through cultural change. *Consulting Psychology Journal: Practice and Research, 48*(2), 104-114.

These senior consulting executives discussed in this article how to coach and develop the senior leadership competencies needed in changing organizational cultures. The authors argued that organizations of the future must understand the linkages between an inclusive culture and organizational success. They will need leaders who can deal with the diversity of the workforce, markets, and suppliers and who can appreciate how these elements will affect strategies, productivity, market penetration, customer service, recruitment costs, turnover rate, and other organizational operations.

According to the authors, barriers to inclusion are rooted in the structures, culture, and institutional dynamics of the organization and may be reinforced by the wider society. As executive coaches, they described their role as being partners with executives in uncovering those systemic barriers, and in helping the executive learn new skills and ways of behaving, managing, interacting, partnering, and doing business.

Five key competencies were defined for the executive coach: (1) the vision to see leaders, followers, and peers as partners each with essential and differentiated roles; (2) the self-assurance not to feel diminished by following another's lead; (3) the ability to see a delegated task as part of the process of implementation and not as a put-down; (4) the ability to contribute information, opinions, and wisdom to the decision-making process without requiring that they be used; and (5) the ability to listen effectively and to ask clarifying questions as part of the process of joining, not as a means to nibble, discount, tear down, or destroy.

The authors suggested several tactics coaches can use to create a learning environment that helps executives overcome awkwardness and discomfort when practicing new skills. Coaches and clients can, for example, develop an organizational imperative that aligns inclusive behaviors with the organization's strategic goals; look for learning and synergy, not perfection; find learning partners for senior executives from all levels of the organization; learn and teach the skills required for tapping diversity; and coach carefully, gently, and honestly, remembering that learning takes courage and change is constant.

***

Kiel, F., Rimmer, E., Wiliams, K., & Doyle, M. (1996). Coaching at the top. *Consulting Psychology Journal: Practice and Research*, 48(2), 67-77.

This article described a highly structured approach to executive coaching designed to build the trust necessary for effecting positive changes in a client. The authors' approach begins with acquiring extensive confidential business and personal information about the executive that provides the core of the executive development process.

The method consists of four steps: (1) building trust by developing an expertise about the individual executive through comprehensive data collection; (2) building commitment to the coaching process within the organization through the executive's immediate boss or sponsor and by explicitly stating the process and goals of the coaching assignment; (3) establishing a holistic coaching approach that permits the executive to see life patterns that may have influenced or affected personal effectiveness; and (4) developing a systems orientation that makes the coach-client relationship primary but also addresses the organization's needs.

The authors suggested a two-year senior executive development plan that includes fact gathering, planning and consolidation, and implementation and development. They cited seven guiding principles to their approach to executive coaching: (1) learners need, but have few opportunities for, continuing development; (2) personal development seldom gets priority; (3) development requires significant self-awareness; (4) self-understanding demands quality feedback; (5) positive individual change has a positive organizational impact; (6) external support facilitates the process; and (7) continuing support is essential to sustain personal and professional growth.

In conclusion the authors presented a case study that illustrated their approach to coaching. They reminded executive coaches to adopt a multiple-systems view of leadership and the organization; to establish clear boundaries of professional conduct; to plan for resistance by working with the executive or the organization to discover any hidden agendas; to embrace flexibility, as creativity plays a significant role in achieving desired outcomes; to maintain momentum through regular contacts with the executive and organizational stakeholders; and to preserve confidentiality so that the executive client retains control of his or her developmental process.

* * *

Kilburg, R. R. (1996). Toward a conceptual understanding and definition of executive coaching. *Consulting Psychology Journal: Practice and Research*, *48*(2), 134-144.

The author, a human resources director for a major university, analyzed the empirical research related to executive coaching. The literature can be clustered into three related areas: research studies; articles emphasizing methods, techniques, or applications in specific situations; and efforts to modify or expand the role of managers to use their leadership in coaching activities.

Although Kilburg noted the lack of empirical research on the actual work of senior practitioners in the executive coaching field, he did distill several concepts from the views of practitioners and researchers. Those frameworks included major components of executive coaching interventions, such as typical avenues for coaching (systems, mediated, and executive); goals of executive coaching; coaching methods and techniques; and factors that can contribute to negative coaching outcomes for the client and the coach.

* * *

Kirkland, K., & Manoogian, S. (1998). *Ongoing feedback: How to get it, how to use it*. Greensboro, NC: Center for Creative Leadership, 21 pages.

This short book provides advice to individuals wanting to obtain and use feedback about their performance. In terms of obtaining feedback, the book focuses on three considerations: who to ask, when to ask, and how to ask. In terms of using the feedback once it has been received, the authors stressed the importance of evaluating the feedback using a self-management model of feedback that helps the receiver determine if the feedback is accurate, if it has value, and if it demands action.

* * *

Koonce, R. (1994). One on one. *Training & Development*, *48*(2), 34-40.

    The author, a corporate communications executive with a management consulting firm, discussed how executive coaching can salvage a star player whose career is in trouble. He noted that organizations have to address such situations because it is too expensive to keep a poorly performing executive on the payroll, it is legally risky to ignore problematic or inappropriate behavior in the workplace, and it is a waste of executive talent.

    The author defined executive coaching as an intensive, short-term process that helps executives address behavior or issues that are impeding their own job effectiveness. Through interviews with executive coaching consultants, he described what executive coaching can provide to clients and developed a four-step coaching process: (1) pre-coaching, a confidential discussion with a senior human resources executive and the boss of the coaching client about specific issues to be addressed by the coaching process; (2) data gathering, a relationship-building effort involving extensive 360-degree assessment instruments; (3) coaching, as designed from the data-gathering stage and working toward building self-awareness and necessary behavioral changes within the client; and (4) follow-up, a period of monitoring and consulting after four to seven months of coaching to see how the executive is doing on his or her own.

∗∗∗

Lary, B. K. (1997). Executive counsel. *Human Resource Executive*, *11*(1), 46-49.

    The writer suggested three reasons for the increased popularity of executive coaches: coaches offer a particular expertise not available inside the company, executives find it easier to confide in an objective outsider, and little time is lost away from the job.

    Lary also defined various components of establishing an executive coaching relationship: setting the level and scope of executive issues appropriate for coaching, determining potential costs of employing a coach, selecting the right executive coach, determining what 360-degree instruments and approaches to use during the coaching process, and defining appropriate outcomes.

    The author argued that corporations can expect several changes in their executives who participate in the coaching process, including: improved interpersonal skills; an improved self-image; an increased ability to manage self and others during periods of conflict and crisis; an increased ability to manage tension created by disparate responsibilities to the organization, family, community, and self; improved self-awareness and understanding, including control of emotions; more tolerance for shortcomings and diversity; improved personal resilience; more flexibility and a propensity to learn and grow; and an improved ability to manage and advance personal career goals and the career goals of others.

***

Levinson, H. (1996). Executive coaching. *Consulting Psychology Journal: Practice and Research, 48*(2), 115-123.

The writer, a psychologist, argued that executive coaching requires the coach to be able to differentiate coaching from psychotherapy, but also to use basic psychological skills and insights combined with a broad and comprehensive understanding of contemporary organizational issues in business or government.

According to the author, the coaching relationship must be a peer relationship. Even though the client is necessarily dependent on the coach for advice, guidance, insights, and even information, he or she should experience coaching as a form of support, rather than as a means of personal change.

The article also defined some of the executive coach's tasks. The coach should help the executive break free from ungratifying, unsatisfying, or conflict-laden work or to help the executive plan for a new or different occupational role. The coach should interview and counsel with a focus on reality problems as well as call attention to repetitive problems that the client may not have recognized (handling achievements, disappointments, and job challenges, for example, or dealing with authority figures, peers, and subordinates).

The coach should assist the executive in taking a serious look at behaviors that may adversely affect relationships. A coach should also assist the executive in understanding and coming to terms with behaviors that cause difficulty and work with the client to learn new skills and approaches.

To illustrate his points, Levinson offered a case study of a 60-year-old CEO and the changes that this executive faced in meeting the new business challenges of a large animal feeds company. Two key themes emerged from this work: the need for executive coaches to be widely informed about management issues, and the need for coaches to understand what is going on politically and economically within an organization and its competitive environment. This knowledge helps build a stronger professional relationship between coaches and senior corporate executives.

***

21

Ludeman, K. (1995). To fill the feedback void. *Training & Development*, *49*(8), 38-41.

As executives move up the corporate ladder, feedback about their performance tends to diminish. This loss can be critical for managers whose performance has become less effective as they rise through the corporate ranks. Skills that were effective at the middle management level may no longer be effective at senior levels (for example, attention to detail can become a drawback at senior levels of management).

In this article the author argued that a combination of assessment, feedback, and strong coaching can provide an executive with the opportunity and motivation to change ineffective behaviors. Coaching tactics discussed included using three feedback tools (a 360-degree assessment, the Myers-Briggs Type Indicator instrument, and the 16 Personal Factors test); sending the 360-degree assessment to between 25 and 40 people who work with the executive (including a superior, peers, direct reports, and individuals the company targets as high-potentials); interviewing six to ten people who work closely with the executive to get more detail about the behaviors associated with the assessment ratings; and meeting the client for a half day to go over the feedback, pinpoint some areas for improvement, and set some goals. After the initial meeting, the coach and client should meet on a regular basis for three to six months. The author also recommended that one of the coaching sessions include the executive's manager as a way of gaining endorsement for making needed changes. Executives might also meet with their direct reports and peers in order to summarize the feedback and to emphasize the commitment to change.

***

Machan, D. (1988, June 13). Sigmund Freud meets Henry Ford. *Forbes*, *14*(13), 120-122.

This article described the efforts of TriSource Group, a consortium of therapist/management consultants that provides traditional therapy to individuals, management consulting to companies, and executive coaching to managers. The group originated in the early 1980s when several psychotherapists noticed that some of their patients wanted to talk about work and career problems. Within this context, the author defined executive coaching as on-the-job counseling designed to help senior executives become more effective managers and overcome career obstacles. Common to these senior executives were such behaviors as being overly demanding and controlling, and impatient with subordinates. The TriSource Group attempted to teach such executives to slow down and become better teachers.

Two case studies with different outcomes were presented in the article. The first case involved a tax-law specialist. This person had just been promoted to managing a large department and was finding himself overwhelmed with paperwork and unresponsive subordinates. Sensing that his job was in jeopardy, he initiated an executive coaching effort and spent two hours per week with a coach for a period of two and a half years. Over this time period, the coach helped him learn to delegate more, to be more specific and demanding with his staff, and to be more precise and decisive with his manager. In the second case, an organization initiated an executive coaching effort for a poorly performing executive, but when the effort failed to improve performance the executive was fired.

*** *

McCafferty, J. (1996, November). Your own personal Vince Lombardi. *CFO: The Magazine for Senior Financial Executives, 12*(11), 93-95.

This article cited a 1995 survey completed by Coach University that indicated there were more than 1,000 full-time coaches in the United States, and that the number of executive coaches would double by the end of 1995. It was also estimated that more than 40,000 corporate executives had participated in executive coaching. The rise in the use of executive coaches was tied to the trend toward flatter organizational structures and multi-company careers. According to the article, many executives feel they lack a support network. This lack is especially keen for financial executives, who frequently deal with sensitive corporate issues.

Several examples and case studies of financial executives receiving executive coaching were described. Financial executives often turn to executive coaches when making the transition from upper-level accountant to top-level executive. For financial executives weaknesses in interpersonal skills and time-management skills are common; many times they lead the executive to seek out an executive coach. However, the article also warned that executive coaching can be overused. The process should be seen as a developmental tool, not a crutch.

Although at one time executive coaching was stigmatized as a sign of weakness among executives who sought the service, the author argued that coaching is now cast in a more positive light and that more executives are being proactive in seeking it out. In matching coach with executive, care should be taken. Coaches have a great variety of backgrounds, education, business experience, and training. The fit between a particular executive and a potential executive coach is extremely important to the success of the process.

At the time of the article, the coaching process was described as lasting from six months to one year at a monthly cost of $250 to $1,000. After an initial session that can last several hours and includes assessment (possibly including 360-degree feedback), most coaches require a half-hour to an hour phone session on a weekly basis.

***

McCauley, C. D., & Douglas, C. A. (1998). Developmental relationships. In C. D. McCauley, R. S. Moxley, & E. Van Velsor (Eds.), *The Center for Creative Leadership handbook of leadership development* (pp. 160-193). San Francisco: Jossey-Bass and Center for Creative Leadership, 481 pages.

This book chapter highlighted the importance of developmental relationships in the leadership development process by describing the various roles that other people play in a manager's development. In addition, the authors suggested both individual and organizational strategies for building, maintaining, and utilizing developmental relationships. Individual strategies for using developmental relationships include seeking out multiple relationships for development; figuring out which roles and people are needed for current development goals; fully utilizing lateral, subordinate, and external relationships (including executive coaches); being open to the view that relationships do not have to be long-term or intense to be developmental; and, during times of transition, reassessing the kind of developmental relationships needed.

Along with describing several types of formal relationships (intentional efforts by organizations to build and facilitate developmental relationships), the authors described executive coaching and provided an example. Executive coaching is used to provide help to chief executives, board members, and senior managers in particular skill areas that have been identified as needing improvement. This type of coaching should be considered when individuals need coaching and have no peers or managers who can provide it or when individuals prefer a concentrated period of coaching by a professional skilled in behavioral change strategies. Potential problems that may arise include the opinions that the experience and skills of the coach may not meet the needs of the executive, that the coaching process may be too expensive, and that the coaching process may undermine others' confidence in the participating executive if the coaching is not kept confidential. The article reinforced the idea that organizations should carefully check the credentials of the potential coach.

***

McCauley, C. D., & Hughes-James, M. W. (1994). *An evaluation of the outcomes of a leadership development program.* Greensboro, NC: Center for Creative Leadership, 89 pages.

This report described the development and evaluation of a leadership development program aimed at school superintendents. The year-long program combined a six-day classroom experience with a long-term plan for working toward goals. After the classroom experience, designed to facilitate self-awareness and goal setting, the participants were matched with an executive facilitator (another superintendent) for guidance, advising, and support, such as might be found in a coaching relationship. The executive facilitator was expected to visit the program participant two to six weeks after the conclusion of the classroom experience and continue contact through additional visits, meetings, or telephone conversations.

After the program had ended, participants were asked to evaluate the relationship as part of an overall evaluation of the entire program. Specifically, the participants were asked to describe the benefits that were derived from the relationship. Eight types of benefits were identified: facilitators (1) provided important experience and expertise, (2) acted as sounding boards for the participants, (3) encouraged the participants to do more reflective thinking, (4) served as role models for the participants, (5) provided feedback about strengths and weaknesses to the participants, (6) worked to keep the participants engaged in the program, (7) provided friendship, and (8) provided encouragement.

∗∗∗

Nakache, P. (1997, July 7). Can you handle the truth about your career? *Fortune Magazine, 136*(1), 208.

The writer focused on the emerging opportunities for using executive coaching and how to use it effectively. She cited three common uses for a coach: (1) to help modify behavior on the job, (2) to help set business and personal goals, and (3) to help put the executive's life in order.

The author argued that coaching is superior to training because it is tailored to the individual's needs. She raised four key issues that guide the decision to hire an executive coach: (1) Is the client open to change? The executive must be ready to accept potentially difficult feedback and make the decision to change. (2) Are the executive and organization realistic about what coaching can achieve? A client should not pin hopes on promised results such as promotions or higher income. (3) Does the client have achievable goals? An executive should guard against setting goals that are too aggressive or potentially conflicting. (4) Is the client prepared to work hard? An executive can only get out of a coaching relationship what he or she puts into it.

The writer concluded by stating that for managers who feel overwhelmed by the idea of hiring an executive coach, a good idea is to look to their superior. Many times a boss can qualify as a coach.

$$* * *$$

O'Brien, M. (1997, April). Executive coaching. *Supervision, 58*(4), 6-8.

The author, president of his own organizational development firm specializing in executive team development and executive coaching, described in this article the methodology he used in executive coaching relationships. He defined executive coaching as a highly confidential one-on-one relationship between an executive and a coach in which the coach helps the executive work on specific problems or issues at work over an extended period of time. A coach helps the executive notice and change thought and behavior patterns that are preventing the best performance.

The author argued that executive coaching should go further than helping executives deal with interpersonal skills. It should also address *intrapersonal* issues, which he defined as what is going on inside the executive's mind that causes interpersonal problems at work.

O'Brien concluded with a brief list of problematic behaviors and attitudes that signal the need for developmental coaching. Potential coaching clients would include executives who frequently get angry or upset with others; deal inappropriately with failure (not admitting error, covering up, or listing excuses); are unable to influence others positively; harbor resentment or unexpressed anger; live an unbalanced lifestyle; refuse to step forward as leaders of change; are overbearing or talk too much and dominate meetings; are unusually withdrawn or uninvolved.

$$* * *$$

Olesen, M. (1996). Coaching today's executives. *Training & Development, 50*(3), 22-27.

The author began this article with a look at how companies are "trying to institutionalize executive coaching" and the many ideas as to how to go about it. She cited organizations like UARCO, Westinghouse, Arthur Andersen, and one unnamed federal systems research and development organization, all of which are designing processes to work with executive talent. She also cited organizations like the Center for Creative Leadership, which has a program developed specifically for assessing leadership potential and developmental concerns for the most senior executives (Leadership at the Peak).

Executive coaching, according to the author, is growing and changing as the needs of executives are changing. The article laid out steps to consider when adopting an executive coaching approach.

First, get corporate endorsement. Second, build a trusted and safe environment to achieve the open and honest communication necessary for a successful coaching effort. Third, convince the executive that a problem exists by providing convincing data at the start of the coaching process. Finally, help executives and organizations understand that coaching deals with subtle issues such as gaining self-clarity and self-awareness.

The author also wrote that organizations should steer clear of formal training. It is better to work with the executive in deciding how he or she would like to get information and experience in dealing with changes.

Other factors about executive coaching efforts for organizations to keep in mind include the use of target dates, deadlines, and reviews. It is human nature to resist change, and executives are no different. Organizations and the coaches they use must also be ready for anything. Often personal issues overlay work issues. When working with executives coaches must be ready and willing to enter arenas they have never entered before.

✶✶✶

Olivero, G., Bane, K. D., & Kopelman, R. E. (1997). Executive coaching as a transfer of training tool: Effects on productivity in a public agency. *Public Personnel Management*, *26*(4), 461-470.

This empirical study examined the impact of executive coaching on the transfer of training. Thirty-one managers (including top-level managers, mid-level managers, and supervisors) at a health agency participated in a three-day interactive management-training workshop that focused on managerial competencies. Eight of the participants were then trained by the author to be executive coaches to the other 23 participants. The coaching emphasized goal setting, collaborative problem solving, practice, feedback, supervisory involvement, evaluation of end results, and public presentation. Each participant was required to design and complete a work-related project after the initial training was completed. Although several limitations of the study were noted, the findings do provide some support for the idea that executive coaching provides a productivity boost over training alone. The author suggested that executive coaching may ensure that knowledge gained during training emerges as skills in the workplace.

***

Peterson, D. B. (1996). Executive coaching at work: The art of one-on-one
change. *Consulting Psychology Journal: Practice and Research, 48*(2),
78-86.

The author defined coaching as "the process of equipping people with
the tools, knowledge, and opportunities they need to develop themselves and
become more effective." He used a case study featuring a female information
technology manager to illustrate five guiding strategies for one-on-one
coaching. (1) Forge a partnership; build trust and understanding so people
want to work with you. (2) Inspire commitment; build insight and motivation
so people focus their energy on goals that matter. (3) Grow skills; build new
competencies to ensure that people know how to do what is required.
(4) Promote persistence; build stamina and discipline so learning lasts on the
job. (5) Shape the environment; build organizational support that rewards
learning and removes barriers.

***

Peterson, D. B., & Hicks, M. D. (1999, February). Strategic coaching: Five
ways to get the most value. *HR Focus*, pp. 7-8.

Although the demand for executive coaching continues, few companies
actually evaluate the business impact of coaching. In this article the authors
suggested five strategies that an organization can employ in order to improve
the return on its coaching investment. First, it is important to provide coaching where the payback is the greatest. Coaching should be implemented when
an organization needs to accelerate the development of key individuals, when
there is a significant increase in the complexity of a key role, when time is
short, and/or when risks are high. Second, it is important that an organization
build a small pool of screened, qualified coaches who are familiar with the
organization's culture and strategic priorities. Third, it is important to evaluate the coach's ability to help executives learn and translate ideas into new
capabilities and stronger performance. Fourth, the organization needs to
carefully match clients with coaches according to well-reasoned criteria.
Organizations typically make coach-client matches based on age, gender, job
history, ethnicity, or personality, but these characteristics typically have little
to do with coaching skills or with the executive's developmental needs.
Finally, organizations must set objectives and evaluate the results of an
executive coaching initiative by determining the goals of a coaching initiative
and determining success or failure based on those objectives.

***

Pilette, P. C., & Wingard, E. (1997). Strengthening the executive's leadership
skills through coaching. In J. E. Lowery (Ed.), *Culture shift: A leader's
guide to managing change in health care* (pp. 187-205). Chicago: Ameri-
can Hospital Association, 256 pages.

This chapter presented an executive coaching model that incorporates
key elements of the coaching process, with the intention of providing an
understanding of what coaching is, how a coach is selected, and the potential
outcomes of the coaching process. Within the framework of their model, the
authors described coaching as involving three activities or elements: reflection, reframing, and rehearsal.

The first element, reflection, begins with the client's evaluation and
assessment. Clients are encouraged to reflect on past experiences and how
previous obstacles were faced and managed in order to identify transferable
skills, put negative emotional experiences in perspective, and identify established patterns of behavior that may be blocking the attainment of goals.

The second element, reframing, involves the recasting of perceptions
and thought processes using assessment tools to help executives see their
strengths and developmental opportunities realistically. Rehearsal, the
model's third element, provides an opportunity for leaders to practice and
learn new behaviors. Rehearsal consists of practicing the behaviors prior to
direct action through such techniques as role-playing.

The authors also identified five essential functions that an executive
coach provides: facilitating, analyzing, diagnosing, mediating, and strategic
planning. Key outcomes from the coaching process include learning to build
and maintain relationships, learning to navigate sensitive political issues,
strategic decision making, learning "best practices," and cultivating leadership capabilities.

* * *

Richard, J. T. (1999). Multimodal therapy: A useful model for the executive
coach. *Counseling Psychology Journal: Practice and Research, 51*(5),
24-30.

This article suggested that executive coaches can use Arnold Lazarus's
multimodal therapy as a model for improving executive performance and for
bringing a more holistic approach to the coaching process. The multimodal
model outlines seven dimensions of personality: behavior, affect, sensation,
imagery, cognition, interpersonal relationships, and drug/biology modality.
The author offered questions that coaches can use during the assessment and
subsequent counseling sessions in order to assess and reassess these seven

dimensions. Assuming that executive coaching is an ongoing process within a developmental context, the client's personality profile could be continually updated.

After the initial assessment, the client and the consultant can work together to plan interventions within each of the seven modalities. Multimodal therapy adds value beyond the use of the contemporary assessment instruments (Myers-Briggs Type Indicator, for example), the author argued, because it can focus on more specific behaviors and problems. Multimodal therapy can also be integrated into a 360-degree assessment.

The author made several distinctions between coaching and therapy (counseling). First, coaching is focused on improving job performance, not on changing behavior related to a diagnosis. Second, coaching is more direct and less process-oriented than traditional therapy. Third, progress in executive coaching is typically measured in concrete performance terms rather than patient self-reports. Fourth, while therapy is almost always done in face-to-face situations, executive coaching typically includes telephone sessions and electronic mail correspondence. Finally, a therapist is usually paid by the patient or the patient's insurance company, but an executive coach is typically paid by the client's organization.

***

Saporito, T. J. (1996). Business-linked executive development: Coaching senior executives. *Consulting Psychology Journal: Practice and Research, 48*(2), 96-103.

The author, a senior vice president of a consulting firm, described a four-stage executive coaching model based on his experience and his position that coaching must link the developmental process to business realities. To do this, he suggested, the executive coach must continually focus on understanding the work of the individual client as well as the unique context and objectives of the organization. Executive coaches must provide practical and directly applicable options and alternatives related to the issues of corporate performance and individual effectiveness if they are to overcome the general skepticism about developmental relationships.

The four-stage model begins with Setting the Foundation. This stage is designed to establish organizational and individual perspectives about the context for the coaching relationship as it relates to organizational requirements, culture, philosophy, and industry. To successfully complete this stage, a coach must answer three questions: What are the organizational imperatives? What are the success factors for the executive's particular role within the organization? What are the behavioral requirements necessary to achieve these success factors?

At stage two, Assessment of the Individual, the coach gathers the data and insights that will form the client's developmental plan. Semiformal interviews about seminal work experiences and 360-degree assessment instruments validate the data. Stage three, Developmental Planning, begins with feedback and then moves to a focus on the client's strengths and those areas in need of development and a discussion about the type of coaching needed for success.

In stage four, Implementation, the client and coach move from defining needs to working on the behaviors, understanding, and perspectives that address development needs and capitalize on strengths.

* * *

Smith, L. (1993, December 27). The executive's new coach. *Fortune*, *128*(16), 126-134.

In this article the author described corporations that use executive coaching, different 360-degree instruments used during the coaching process, the cost involved, and the levels of management where coaching is usually used.

The article mainly focused on four executive coaching theories and techniques, presented in order from the least intrusive and least expensive to the most probing and most expensive.

The first theory, dubbed "The Line Coach," is a behavioral-based approach that highlights the coach's interview and conversation skills as close attention is paid to the client's words, facial expressions, and tone of voice.

In the technique the article called "The Clairvoyant," an executive coach uses a series of subtle games to identify the client's compulsions and phobias that adversely impact his or her effectiveness. The "Jump School" theory and technique focuses on the Awareness Program for Executive Excellence (APEX)®, a program developed by the Center for Creative Leadership. This intense and analytical look at an executive's leadership style uses a combination of in-depth interviews and assessment instruments to help the executive focus on the four or five defects in leadership style that most need changing or attention. A coaching plan is then devised and an executive coach works with the executive during the transformation process.

In the most probing technique, referred to as "The Submarine," it takes more than two and a half months to collect data on the executive client. A process of interviews includes three two-hour sessions with the executive client; as many as 30 one-and-a-half-hour sessions with subordinates, peers, and superiors; and about 15 one-and-a-half-hour sessions with friends and family members, including parents and children over 12 years of age. Coaching follows the feedback twice a month for one-and-a-half years. The coaching firm that uses this technique admits that this type of scrutiny is intended only for top-level leaders.

***

Snyder, A. (1995). Executive coaching: The new solution. *Management Review, 84*(3), 29-32.

The author began this article by describing the growth in the executive coaching field, which he attributed to an improved economy, the movement away from downsizing, and the need for organizations to develop managers who can work together into the future.

Further, the article outlined rationales for using an executive coach. One, coaching can help executives correct behaviors that may have developed during the course of a career and that may have worked in the past but are problematic for future development. Two, coaching and its accompanying use of 360-degree assessments provides ample feedback along four critical perspectives: positive and expected, positive and unexpected, negative and expected, and negative and unexpected (the most difficult perspective to accommodate). Three, coaching can help executives develop a practical style of applying their skills and can help them break through barriers that threaten to make goals into pipe dreams.

***

Sperry, L. (1993, June). Working with executives: Consulting, counseling and coaching. *Individual Psychology, 49*(2), 257-266.

The author used this article to explore and propose applications of research and clinical findings from clinical psychology, psychiatry, and medicine to the subject of working with executives. Overall, the article described how a consultant with psychological training can respond to an executive's need for consulting, coaching, and counseling services.

Sperry defined *executives* as differing from other senior managers in a company by how they envision global and long-term consequences of any prospect or alternative. He suggested that this quality requires an openness to thinking about the world in new ways, the capacity to deal with ambiguity and complex issues, a strong desire to live and work passionately, a reliance on personal judgment, and the ability and will to exploit personal potential.

Sperry focused on three support roles for those working with executives: executive consulting, executive counseling and psychotherapy, and executive coaching.

In the role of executive consultant, the coach serves as a sounding board and advisor during a process initiated by the executive. In this role the consultant expects to increase the effectiveness of the executive as a manager and as a person; help to integrate information, providing not only perspectives and objectivity but keen insights into problems with people; and create an environment where the executive can work out ideas and perspectives to become more effective before meeting the scrutiny of more critical audiences. The relationship between the executive and the executive consultant should be professional and friendly (without developing into friendship) but not therapeutic.

In the area of executive counseling and psychotherapy, Sperry argued that time-limited dynamic approaches and cognitive therapy are preferred modes of treatment for executives. In most forms of psychotherapy, the clinician may function primarily in a process-oriented and nondirective role; an executive counselor may instead emphasize more immediately practical concerns. The author noted the similarities between consulting and counseling: confidentiality, for example, and the context of a close, collaborative relationship.

For the executive coaching role, the author contended that the primary duty is the teaching of skills in the context of a personal relationship with the learner. The executive coach provides feedback on the executive's interpersonal relations and skills using a variety of techniques and instruments, such as assessments and interviews.

∗∗∗

Strickland, K. (1997). Executive coaching: Helping valued executives fulfill their potential. In A. J. Pickman (Ed.), *Special challenges in career management: Counselor perspectives* (pp. 203-212). Mahwah, NJ: Lawrence Erlbaum Associates, 264 pages.

Using examples, three varieties of executive coaching were described in this book chapter: (1) coaching that helps an executive recognize undesirable behaviors and cultivate existing skills in order to increase effectiveness, (2) "fix-it" coaching that targets a specific behavior that is causing managerial conflict, and (3) simple career-path assessment and guidance. Executive coaching is compared to personal training in that coaches work one-on-one with clients to achieve results. The author emphasized that executive coaching is a more cost-effective solution to management problems than employee termination.

At its most basic level, the role of an executive coach is to help the executive acknowledge and deal with realities that might otherwise be avoided, denied, or accepted with resignation. To achieve this result, coaching moves through at least six tasks, including listening, clarifying, mediating, educating, training, and follow-up. A variety of assessment tools can play a role in the executive coaching process.

Clients benefit from executive coaching in a number of ways. For example, many unspoken rules about appropriate executive style accompany top-level positions. An executive coach can help an individual decode those rules and understand what is expected of him or her in terms of behaviors and attitudes. Second, strengths can become weaknesses as executives climb the corporate ladder. An executive coach can help clients understand these ironies and modify their behavior. Third, executive coaches can help clients change perspective and understanding without sacrificing their competence or self-esteem. Finally, as individuals are promoted, they may lack information about expectations. An executive coach can help an individual identify and understand the expectations placed on top management.

The author cited three important insights into effective executive coaching. First, clear and honest communication between executive and coach can solve almost any issue; facilitating good communication is at the heart of executive coaching. Second, executive coaches need to help clients recognize and be comfortable with themselves, and help them understand that they have choices in every area of their lives. Finally, the potential for growth and change is immeasurable when coaching is performed effectively.

* * *

Thach, L., & Heinselman, T. (1999, March). Executive coaching defined. *Training & Development*, pp. 35-39.

Aimed at human resources professionals interested in implementing executive coaching strategies within their organizations, this article outlined the major types of executive coaching, the potential benefits and drawbacks, and strategies for making the most out of executive coaching relationships. The three major types of executive coaching described were feedback coaching, in-depth development coaching, and content coaching.

Feedback coaching refers to the process of giving feedback to a manager (a 360-degree assessment, for example) and helping the participant create a development plan to address specific needs. This type of coaching typically lasts from one to six months and is comprised of several meetings or conversations between the coach and the participant.

In-depth development coaching typically lasts longer than feedback coaching (usually six to twelve months) and involves a close relationship between a coach and a leader. The process involves an in-depth assessment (using multiple assessment instruments, for example, coupled with interviews with the executive's staff and associates and the coach's observations), an intensive feedback session lasting up to two days, and follow-up meetings to set goals and assess progress.

Content coaching was defined as a very specific intervention designed to provide leaders with knowledge in a specific content area (global marketing, finance, or operations in a specific industry, for example). Content coaching usually involves a series of sessions and may involve assessment, the assignment and discussion of books and articles, role-playing, and video-taping.

Benefits of executive coaching include direct one-on-one assistance, accommodation to the leader's schedule, fast results, and a high return on investment. Potential pitfalls include a lack of integration with the rest of the organization's leadership development strategy, skepticism on the part of participants, a lack of clarity regarding the type of coaching needed, and a poor match between client and coach. The article said human resource professionals should avoid contracting with coaches who have no industry experience, who insist on using their own coaching model and assessment instruments, who have done only outplacement work, and who take too much credit for past coaching results.

The authors identified several elements that can increase the effectiveness of executive coaching relationships, including accountability (making the executive accountable for following through with the process), integration with other human resource systems, modeling by top management, and confidentiality between the coach and client.

✳✳✳

Tobias, L. L. (1996). Coaching executives. *Consulting Psychology Journal: Practice and Research, 48*(2), 87-95.

This consulting psychologist defined coaching as an ongoing process of activities tailored to an individual's current issue or relevant problem. He suggested that coaching allows an individual to gain support, encouragement, and feedback as new approaches are tried and new behaviors are practiced. In the end, a coach provides the executive a climate for continuous learning through the change process.

Tobias noted other ways coaches can help executives. They can work with individuals who are experiencing conflict-laden relationships with peers, authorities, internal customers, or others; they can help an executive enhance his or her style, future options, and organizational impact; they can provide a confidential relationship within which executives are allowed to freely discuss delicate issues, shed their defenses, and explore blind spots, biases, and shortcomings; they can help the executive elicit feedback or manage the process in which feedback is given; and they can help the executive focus on specific behavioral changes as well as gain insight into the factors underlying problem behaviors.

Tobias drew a critical distinction between the coaching and consulting roles: coaching focuses more on the individual, but consulting focuses primarily on the organization. He also suggested that coaching may be done both within and outside the confines of an ongoing consulting relationship. However, Tobias noted, if the coaching relationship is the only contact the coach has with the organization, the coach's perspective may be so limited by an absence of organizational context that it is difficult to readily identify problems or to quickly develop effective interventions.

Tobias concluded with a description of his coaching process and a case study of a 44-year-old Fortune 100 technical manager who was excellent at his craft but whose controlling management style got in the way of R&D creativity.

✳✳✳

Tristram, C. (1996, Oct.-Nov.). Wanna be a player? Get a coach. *Fast Company*, pp. 145-150.

This business writer focused on how executive coaches help executives become better leaders. She warned, however, that entering into a coaching relationship is not for the faint-hearted. "Executive coaches are not for the meek," she wrote. "They're for people who value unambiguous feedback. If coaches have one thing in common, it's that they are ruthlessly results-oriented. Executive coaching isn't therapy. It's product development, with *you* as the product."

The author presented three coaching scenarios with comments from the executives and the coaches, and her own comments about the coaching method used in each scenario. Additionally, she gave five brief reports: how an executive reacted to a company-hired coach showing up on his doorstep without prior consent; how to get the most from a coach; an executive's hiring of a coach from outside without organizational consent or control; a story about finding the right coach; and a short list of resources.

***

Waldroop, J., & Butler, T. (1996, Nov.-Dec.). The executive as coach.
   Harvard Business Review, 74(6), 111-117.

   Although this article was written for the executive in a coaching role, it
is also applicable to the external coaching professional. The authors, business
psychologists at Harvard Business School, argued that the goal of coaching is
the same as the goal of good management: to make the most of an organization's resources.

   The authors defined coaching as "understanding someone's problem
behavior in context, deciding whether the problem can be remedied, and
encouraging the person to adapt. Coaching—helping to change the behaviors
that threaten to derail a valued manager—is often the best way to help that
manager succeed."

   The article described several scenarios and approaches to managerial
and organizational coaching issues. Of special significance were the characteristics of an effective coach. The coach should adopt the approach of
teacher, not competitor; should observe first in order to understand, and only
after understanding provide critical feedback for personal improvement;
should reflect before acting and encourage clients to do the same; should
accept the ultimate goal of coaching as improving the client's business
performance, focusing less on the immediate task and more on the long-term
results; should know when to provide support and be able to structure a
collaborative relationship through regular meetings.

   The authors also outlined an operational plan for a one-on-one coaching
session and concluded by saying that coaching must be imaginative enough to
consider many solutions to difficult problems. In their words, "coaching must
reflect the complexity and difficulty of genuine efforts to change behavior."

***

Witherspoon, R., & White, R. P. (1996). Executive coaching: A continuum of
   roles. *Consulting Psychology Journal: Practice and Research, 48*(2), 124-
   133.

   This article reflected on the authors' experiences with four different
executive coaching objectives. They defined these objectives as coaching for
skills, which focuses on the client's specific task; coaching for performance,
which focuses on a person's present job; coaching for development, which
focuses on a person's future job; and coaching for the executive's agenda,
which focuses on the executive's development needs or issues. The article

provided a thorough discussion of each coaching objective and gave examples of situations, processes for coaching, and results for those objectives.

The authors concluded by describing what different coaching roles, as defined by objective, have in common. First, all executive coaching involves action learning. Second, successful coaching involves working in partnership with executives. Finally, the coaching process across all of these roles involves four steps: commitment to the coaching contract by the organization, the executive, and the executive's superior; an assessment phase to set a goal or define a problem; action steps to build competence, confidence, and commitment that will help the executive change the way he or she thinks and performs; and measuring for continuous improvements to ensure that actions achieve desired results. An expanded version of the article was published as *Four Essential Ways That Coaching Can Help Executives* (Witherspoon, R., & White, R. P. [1997]. Greensboro, NC: Center for Creative Leadership, 38 pages).

***

Young, D. P., & Dixon, N. M. (1996). *Helping leaders take effective action: A program evaluation.* Greensboro, NC: Center for Creative Leadership, 58 pages.

This report described the evaluation of a leadership development program, LeaderLab®, developed by the Center for Creative Leadership. The six-month program includes two separate weeks of classroom activity each followed by three months of implementation. Each participant is matched with a *process advisor*, who serves as the participant's coach during the six-month period. These coaches are individuals with a variety of backgrounds, including clinical psychology, counseling, organizational change and development, career development and counseling, and management/leadership development. The role of process advisor was created to be a process expert (giving advice based on knowledge of change and development processes) as opposed to a content expert (giving advice based on knowledge of a specific industry or organization).

Fifty-one individuals who participated in LeaderLab also participated in an evaluation three to four months after completing the program. Their evaluation consisted of telephone interviews that probed their observations about the effectiveness of the program and its components. Some of the participants' co-workers shared in the evaluation by completing questionnaires that assessed the participants' effectiveness before and after the program. As part of the evaluation, the participants were asked to rank the program components in terms of the degree to which each component helped them take more effective action. Process advisors received the highest ratings of all program components. All of the participants interviewed indicated that the process advisors had been helpful. They went on to say that they perceived process advisors as being objective and having positive regard for the participants, which played an important role in the success of the relationships.

About Executive Coaching

Executive Coaching Defined

No single clear statement emerges from the executive coaching litera-ture to define the profession of executive coaching. Attempts to define the field are shaded and in some cases prejudiced by the authors' educational and professional disciplines, training, and the kind of consulting, psychotherapy, or coaching experiences with which they are familiar. Notwithstanding, any practitioners wishing to establish themselves as executive coaches must clearly lay out and communicate the roles, responsibilities, confidential practices, and relationships they want to build and foster with client compa-nies and executives.

Richard R. Kilburg (1996) makes a valiant effort to form a working definition of coaching from the available literature:

> Executive coaching is defined as a helping relationship formed between a client who has managerial authority and responsibility in an organiza-tion and a consultant who uses a wide variety of behavioral techniques and methods to help the client achieve a mutually identified set of goals to improve his or her professional performance and personal satisfac-tion and, consequently, to improve the effectiveness of the client's organization with a formally defined coaching agreement.

Kilburg's definition is clear enough, but is not likely to fit on a business card. More to the point, such a detailed, complex definition is not likely to help an executive coach create the ground rules for a coach-client relationship that can achieve the desired developmental effect. It may be more useful to view executive coaching as an ongoing relationship with a client that focuses on life purpose, vision, and goals using the process of inquiry and personal discovery (Lary, 1997). Executive coaching is understanding someone's problem behavior in context, deciding whether the problem can be remedied, and encouraging the person to change behaviors that threaten to derail him or her (Waldroop & Butler, 1996). Within the scope of that relationship and during the coaching process the coach can play different roles as needed.

It is not necessary, for example, for the executive coach to have all the knowledge required to solve a particular problem. Instead the coach should have the objectivity necessary to stand outside of the problem, and the agility to assist the executive in recognizing what is missing and what needs to be done (Altier, 1989). That guidance and support is the added value an executive coach brings to the coaching process. The process is designed to help the executive focus on issues such as identifying and modifying the impact of an executive's management style on individuals and teams, more rapidly and effectively adapting to change, establishing individual development needs, and the key dimensions of executive performance (Diedrich, 1996). Through the coach-client developmental relationship, the executive coach assists the executive in learning how to join and work with other leaders (Katz & Miller, 1996).

Reduced to its essence, executive coaching is the process of equipping people with the tools, knowledge, and opportunities they need to develop themselves and become more effective (Peterson, 1996). Executive coaching involves the teaching of skills in the context of a personal relationship with the learner, providing feedback on the executive's interpersonal relations and skills (Sperry, 1993). An ongoing series of activities tailored to the individual's current issues or relevant problem is designed by the coach to assist the executive in maintaining a consistent, confident focus as he or she tunes strengths and manages shortcomings (Tobias, 1996). Coaching is designed to help executives become better, more nimble business leaders (Tristram, 1996).

Some writers view executive coaching as a short-term activity designed to improve specific managerial competencies or solve specific problems (Hall, Otazo, & Hollenbeck, 1999). This intensive, short-term process helps executives address behaviors or issues that are impeding their own job effectiveness (Koonce, 1994).

Other writers point to the effectiveness of a long-term relationship. To make the coach-executive pairing work, especially if it is carried out over many months, the role of coach must embody strict confidentiality. Over an extended period of time the executive must feel free to voice doubt and try new perspectives and behaviors that the coach can observe and comment on, noticing and suggesting changes in thought and behavioral patterns that prevent the best performance (O'Brien, 1997).

Whether the coach works with the client for a short time or maintains contact over many months, an essential ingredient to the coaching role is managing the one-on-one interactions between coach and executive (Judge & Cowell, 1997). This on-the-job counseling helps senior executives become more effective managers and overcome career obstacles (Machan, 1988).

Taken together, these rules, responsibilities, goals, and processes can be summarized this way: The executive coach is an external consultant who, in a confidential, highly personal learning process, works with an executive on a regular basis for one or more specific functions: to improve the executive's managerial skills, to correct serious performance problems, or to facilitate long-term development in preparation for a future leadership role or a top corporate function. The executive coach helps the client learn and teaches the client how to learn (Witherspoon & White, 1996).

An effective executive coach can be defined not just by the characteristics that such a role demands, but also by the goals and techniques he or she provides that are essential to the process.

- A confidential, professional, and trusting learning environment
- Assistance, focus, support, encouragement, honest feedback, and objectivity
- One-on-one interactions and personal training to help the executive learn skills
- Opportunities for developmental experiences that enhance executive performance
- Helping the executive reflect on and learn from leadership and managerial experiences
- Equipping the executive with the knowledge and opportunities required to build the self-assurance and confidence that allows him or her to learn from others and from experience in a continuing developmental journey
- Helping the executive gain the desire to focus and develop a sense of purpose, vision, and goals for personal and professional life

Executive coaches can be effective agents to executive development. They are in a unique position to assist leaders in business, education, health care, nonprofit, religious, and public service organizations in reaching their professional goals, in learning to work more effectively with a diverse population, and in building work environments that foster learning, growth, and development. A working definition of *executive coaching* gives its practitioners the standing necessary to accomplish such difficult work; it also helps to communicate the goals and build the organizational support for this kind of developmental relationship.

The Coaching Process

What is a typical coaching process? What are the steps that comprise an executive coaching process? In attempting to answer these questions, several authors have put forth models or frameworks. Their approaches range from general and simplistic to detailed and complex. At a basic level, however, the

literature reflects a coaching process comprised of several components that
are consistent across most executive coaching relationships.

For example, one could list the essential components of the coaching
process as a referral, introductory meeting, assessment, setting the developmental agenda, and follow-up counseling (Hayes, 1997). These five steps are
sometimes trimmed to four, leaving out the setting of a developmental agenda
(Koonce, 1994), or leaving out details about following up with the client
(Saporito, 1996). If one focuses on just the behavioral changes that an executive coach might guide, the process might be described in even fewer steps
that concentrate on problem solving (Pilette & Wingard, 1997).

Accepting these varied views of the coaching process, it is useful to
concentrate on the similarities. From this perspective, most executive coaching relationships are comprised of four parts. The process begins with an
initial meeting designed to establish the goals of the coaching process and set
the foundation for the rest of the process. This initial meeting may be with the
client or with other key players (bosses, human resource executives, senior
executives), depending on who initiates or makes the decision to implement
an executive coaching program.

The second step is an assessment phase during which the coach builds a
relationship with the client and gathers information about the client's
strengths, weaknesses, and developmental opportunities. The coach will
employ such assessment tools as 360-degree-feedback instruments, interviews, and personality instruments. Typically, the coach will gather this
information from multiple sources, including the client, peers, direct reports,
supervisors, family members, and friends.

The third stage of the process is the heart of coaching itself. Typically
this includes providing assessment feedback, building self-awareness for
making needed behavioral changes, and planning a developmental path. The
final stage of the coaching process includes the implementation of the developmental planning and a period of follow-up monitoring and consulting.

These four stages encompass the basic elements of the coaching process, but some of the current literature proposes more complex models. The
details of these models may include recommending specific kinds of assessment instruments for use during the data-gathering stage and how those
instruments should be used (Ludeman, 1995).

Other works have further delineated the coaching process by identifying
the types of executives who participate in executive coaching and describing
the coaching process for each of these types of executives (Judge & Cowell,
1997).

Similarly, Strickland (1997) identifies three varieties of the executive coaching process, each of which can be useful for a specific developmental issue. Different types of coaching processes can also be illustrated by strategy and tactics (Thach & Heinselman, 1999).

Goals and Outcomes of Executive Coaching

Traditionally the goals of executive coaching relationships have been fairly specific and have focused on preventing executive derailment (Ludeman, 1995; Machan, 1988; McCauley & Douglas, 1998; Sperry, 1993; Waldroop & Butler, 1996). The coaching process may address a specific behavior that is causing managerial conflict (Strickland, 1997), be designed to improve specific managerial competencies or to solve specific problems (Douglas & McCauley, 1997; Hall, Otazo, & Hollenbeck, 1999), or help executives address behaviors or issues that are impeding job effectiveness (Koonce, 1994).

Beyond its traditional goal of addressing a performance problem and preventing derailment, executive coaching increasingly seeks to enhance the performance of high-potential executives (Judge & Cowell, 1997). The goals of executive coaching are shifting and broadening as more and more executives seek out coaching for a variety of different reasons.

Several authors have described these evolving goals in different ways. Most of the goals revolve around increased competence and self-esteem (Koonce, 1994; Peterson, 1996; Witherspoon & White, 1996). These improved competencies range from an increased ability to handle uncertainty (Altier, 1989) to higher confidence while performing job tasks (Beckhard, 1997) to a better use of work experience in achieving career goals (Hamilton, 1996).

Individual executives have their reasons for seeking a coaching relationship, and organizations have expectations as well (Lary, 1997). The lessons and skills learned through the coaching process can translate to better management by enhancing an executive's ability to navigate sensitive political issues, strengthening strategic decision making, and by opening a window onto organizational and self-explorations (Hall, Otazo, & Hollenbeck, 1999; Pilette & Wingard, 1997).

Impact of Executive Coaching

Before deciding whether or not to engage an executive coach, an organization or an individual executive must understand the impact of executive coaching on individuals and on organizations. The lack of published empirical studies makes such an understanding difficult. Only three published studies that specifically examined the impact of executive coaching on performance and attitudes were found in the literature.

That caveat aside, two general observations can be made about the impact of executive coaching. One, it appears that executive coaching can be very useful in helping executives carry what they learn in training situations, such as leadership development programs, to the workplace and to put those lessons into practice (Olivero, Bane, & Kopelman, 1997). If that observation bears out, it means that executive coaching, coupled with management and leadership training, can boost productivity and help build leadership competencies.

Second, in the context of a leadership development program, an executive coaching component plays an important role in supporting the changes in behavior and skills that executives must make to further their leadership abilities for the organization and for their personal career advancement. The objectivity that an executive coach brings to a developmental opportunity is helpful to managers seeking to make necessary and sometimes difficult changes in attitudes, work habits, perspectives, and interpersonal relationships (McCauley & Hughes-James, 1994; Young & Dixon, 1996).

These observations, though promising, are limited to the lack of empirical research into the impact of executive coaching related to its intended outcomes. Further, very little is known about the relationships between executive coaching, individual outcomes, and organizational outcomes. More study is needed in these areas before a clear judgment about coaching effectiveness, coaching tactics, and organizational support for coaching initiatives can be made.

Implications and Future Needs of Executive Coaching

The future of executive coaching as a legitimate and effective professional service depends on credible empirical data that support its effectiveness as a developmental tool for executive talent. Some of that work is currently underway. Capable and professional people in several disciplines (psychology, behavioral science, social work, business management, education, counseling, and organizational development) are seeking ways to collect, study, and interpret that information. As that work continues, and as the executive coach profession continues to grow (both from the practitioner perspective and from the demands from organizations), we look forward to answers and insights into some of the key questions that may affect the future of executive coaching:

- What is the effect of executive coaching?
- What executive coaching characteristics are needed to ensure professional and effective interactions?
- With the number of professionals referring to themselves as "executive coaches" rapidly increasing, are professional standards or guidelines for coaches and the coaching process needed? Would this require certification or licensing?
- What are the ethical implications of executive coaching initiatives? What are the issues in regard to individual and organizational confidentiality? How should assessment data be used in such a developmental relationship?
- How is executive coaching different from other developmental relationships such as executive consulting, executive counseling, and psychotherapy?

The answers to these questions are important not just for coaches and their executive clients, but also for organizations. It is also important for organizations to understand the skills and professional competencies they require from their executives so that effective executive coaching initiatives can be implemented (Brotman, Liberi, & Wasylyshyn, 1998).

We hope this publication can serve in some small way as a catalyst to the empirical research necessary to advance the field of executive coaching. We want to encourage researchers and writers working in the area of executive coaching to continue to share the lessons of their experiences and their work. We also hope that executive coaching practitioners will use this book to build their professional understanding and competency in a field that promises to deliver developmental benefits to leaders worldwide.

Author Index

Title Index

Leadership in Action

*A publication of the
Center for Creative Leadership and
Jossey-Bass Publishers*

Martin Wilcox, Editor

Leadership in Action is a bimonthly newsletter that aims to help practicing leaders and those who train and develop practicing leaders by providing them with insights gained in the course of CCL's educational and research activities. It also aims to provide a forum for the exchange of information and ideas between practitioners and CCL staff and associates.

The annual subscription price for *Leadership in Action* is $99.00 for individuals and $124.00 for institutions. To order, please contact Customer Service, Jossey-Bass, Inc., Publishers, 350 Sansome Street, San Francisco, CA 94104-1342. Telephone: 888/378-2537 or 415/433-1767; fax: 800/605-2665. See the Jossey-Bass Web site at www.josseybass.com

CENTER FOR CREATIVE LEADERSHIP PUBLICATIONS LIST

NEW RELEASES

IDEAS INTO ACTION GUIDEBOOKS

Ongoing Feedback: How to Get It, How to Use It Kirkland & Manoogian (1998, Stock #400) $8.95*

Reaching Your Development Goals McCauley & Martineau (1998, Stock #401) $8.95

Becoming a More Versatile Learner Dalton (1998, Stock #402) $8.95

Giving Feedback to Subordinates Buron & McDonald-Mann (1999, Stock #403) $8.95*

Three Keys to Development: Using Assessment, Challenge, and Support to Drive Your Leadership
Browning & Van Velsor (1999, Stock #404) $8.95

Feedback That Works: How to Build and Deliver Your Message Weitzel (2000, Stock #405) $8.95*

Communicating Across Cultures Prince & Hoppe (2000, Stock #406) $8.95

Learning From Life: Turning Life's Lessons into Leadership Experience Ruderman & Ohlott
(2000, Stock #407) $8.95

Keeping Your Career on Track: Twenty Success Strategies Chappelow & Leslie (2001, Stock #408) $8.95

Preparing for Development: Making the Most of Formal Leadership Programs Martineau &
Johnson (2001, Stock #409) $8.95

Choosing Executives: A Research Report on the Peak Selection Simulation Deal, Sessa, & Taylor
(1999, Stock #183) $20.00*

Coaching for Action: A Report on Long-term Advising in a Program Context Guthrie (1999,
Stock #181) $20.00*

The Complete Inklings: Columns on Leadership and Creativity Campbell (1999, Stock #343) $30.00

Discovering the Leader in You Lee & King (2001, Stock #2067) $32.95

Executive Coaching: An Annotated Bibliography Douglas & Morley (2000, Stock #347) $20.00

Executive Selection: Strategies for Success Sessa & Taylor (2000, Stock #2057) $34.95*

Geographically Dispersed Teams: An Annotated Bibliography Sessa, Hansen, Prestridge, &
Kossler (1999, Stock #346) $20.00

High-Performance Work Organizations: Definitions, Practices, and an Annotated Bibliography
Kirkman, Lowe, & Young (1999, Stock #342) $20.00

The Human Side of Knowledge Management: An Annotated Bibliography Mayer (2000,
Stock #349) $20.00

Internalizing Strengths: An Overlooked Way of Overcoming Weaknesses in Managers Kaplan
(1999, Stock #182) $15.00

Leadership and Spirit Moxley (1999, Stock #2035) $32.95

Leadership Resources: A Guide to Training and Development Tools (8th ed.) Schwartz & Gimbel
(2000, Stock #348) $49.95*

Positive Turbulence: Developing Climates for Creativity, Innovation, and Renewal
Gryskiewicz (1999, Stock #2031) $32.95

Selecting International Executives: A Suggested Framework and Annotated Bibliography
London & Sessa (1999, Stock #345) $20.00

Workforce Reductions: An Annotated Bibliography Hickok (1999, Stock #344) $20.00

BEST-SELLERS

Breaking Free: A Prescription for Personal and Organizational Change Noer (1997, Stock #271) $25.00

Breaking the Glass Ceiling: Can Women Reach the Top of America's Largest Corporations?
(Updated Edition) Morrison, White, & Van Velsor (1992, Stock #236A) $13.00

The Center for Creative Leadership Handbook of Leadership Development McCauley, Moxley,
& Van Velsor (Eds.) (1998, Stock #201) $70.00*

CEO Selection: A Street-smart Review Hollenbeck (1994, Stock #164) $12.50*

Choosing 360: A Guide to Evaluating Multi-rater Feedback Instruments for Management
Development Van Velsor, Leslie, & Fleenor (1997, Stock #334) $15.00*

Eighty-eight Assignments for Development in Place Lombardo & Eichinger (1989, Stock #136) $15.00*

Enhancing 360-degree Feedback for Senior Executives: How to Maximize the Benefits and
Minimize the Risks Kaplan & Palus (1994, Stock #160) $7.50*

Evolving Leaders: A Model for Promoting Leadership Development in Programs Palus & Drath
(1995, Stock #165) $15.00

Executive Selection: A Research Report on What Works and What Doesn't Sessa, Kaiser, Taylor, & Campbell (1998, Stock #179) $30.00*
Feedback to Managers (3rd Edition) Leslie & Fleenor (1998, Stock #178) $30.00*
Four Essential Ways that Coaching Can Help Executives Witherspoon & White (1997, Stock #175) $10.00
High Flyers: Developing the Next Generation of Leaders McCall (1997, Stock #293) $27.95
How to Design an Effective System for Developing Managers and Executives Dalton & Hollenbeck (1996, Stock #158) $15.00*
If I'm In Charge Here, Why Is Everybody Laughing? Campbell (1984, Stock #205) $9.95*
If You Don't Know Where You're Going You'll Probably End Up Somewhere Else Campbell (1974, Stock #203) $9.95*
International Success: Selecting, Developing, and Supporting Expatriate Managers Wilson & Dalton (1998, Stock #180) $15.00*
The Lessons of Experience: How Successful Executives Develop on the Job McCall, Lombardo, & Morrison (1988, Stock #211) $27.50
Making Common Sense: Leadership as Meaning-making in a Community of Practice Drath & Palus (1994, Stock #156) $15.00
Managing Across Cultures: A Learning Framework Wilson, Hoppe, & Sayles (1996, Stock #173) $15.00
Maximizing the Value of 360-degree Feedback Tornow, London, & CCL Associates (1998, Stock #295) $44.95*
Perspectives on Dialogue: Making Talk Developmental for Individuals and Organizations Dixon (1996, Stock #168) $20.00
Preventing Derailment: What To Do Before It's Too Late Lombardo & Eichinger (1989, Stock #138) $25.00
The Realities of Management Promotion Ruderman & Ohlott (1994, Stock #157) $7.50*
Selected Research on Work Team Diversity Ruderman, Hughes-James, & Jackson (Eds.) (1996, Stock #326) $24.95
Should 360-degree Feedback Be Used Only for Developmental Purposes? Bracken, Dalton, Jako, McCauley, Pollman, with Preface by Hollenbeck (1997, Stock #335) $15.00*
Take the Road to Creativity and Get Off Your Dead End Campbell (1977, Stock #204) $9.95*
Twenty-two Ways to Develop Leadership in Staff Managers Eichinger & Lombardo (1990, Stock #144) $15.00

BIBLIOGRAPHIES
Formal Mentoring Programs in Organizations: An Annotated Bibliography Douglas (1997, Stock #332) $20.00
Management Development through Job Experiences: An Annotated Bibliography McCauley & Brutus (1998, Stock #337) $10.00
Selection at the Top: An Annotated Bibliography Sessa & Campbell (1997, Stock #333) $20.00*
Succession Planning: An Annotated Bibliography Eastman (1995, Stock #324) $20.00*
Using 360-degree Feedback in Organizations: An Annotated Bibliography Fleenor & Prince (1997, Stock #338) $15.00*

SPECIAL PACKAGES
Executive Selection Package (Stock #710C; includes 157, 164, 179, 180, 183, 333, 345, 2057) $100.00
Feedback Guidebook Package (Stock #724; includes 400, 403, 405) $17.95
Human Resources Professionals Information Package (Stock #717C; includes 136, 158, 179, 180, 181, 201, 324, 334, 348—includes complimentary copy of guidebook 407) $150.00
Personal Growth, Taking Charge, and Enhancing Creativity (Stock #231; includes 203, 204, 205) ... $25.00
The 360 Collection (Stock #720C; includes 160, 178, 295, 334, 335, 338—includes complimentary copy of guidebook 400) $100.00

Discounts are available. Please write for a Resources catalog. Address your request to: Publication, Center for Creative Leadership, P.O. Box 26300, Greensboro, NC 27438-6300, 336-545-2810, or fax to 336-282-3284. Purchase your publications from our online bookstore at **www.ccl.org/ publications**. All prices subject to change.

*Indicates publication is also part of a package.

ORDER FORM

Or e-mail your order via the Center's online bookstore at www.ccl.org

Name _____ Title _____

Organization _____

Mailing Address _____
(street address required for mailing)

City/State/Zip _____

Telephone _____ FAX _____
(telephone number required for UPS mailing)

Quantity	Stock No.	Title	Unit Cost	Amount

CCL's Federal ID Number
is 237-07-9591.

Subtotal	
Shipping and Handling (add 6% of subtotal with a $4.00 minimum; add 40% on all international shipping)	
NC residents add 6% sales tax; CA residents add 7.5% sales tax; CO residents add 6% sales tax	
TOTAL	

METHOD OF PAYMENT
(ALL orders for less than $100 must be PREPAID.)

❑ Check or money order enclosed (payable to Center for Creative Leadership).

❑ Purchase Order No. _____ (Must be accompanied by this form.)

❑ Charge my order, plus shipping, to my credit card:
      ❑ American Express ❑ Discover ❑ MasterCard ❑ Visa

ACCOUNT NUMBER:_____ EXPIRATION DATE: MO.____ YR.____

NAME OF ISSUING BANK: _____

SIGNATURE _____

❑ Please put me on your mailing list.

Publication • Center for Creative Leadership • P.O. Box 26300
Greensboro, NC 27438-6300
336-545-2810 • FAX 336-282-3284

Client Priority Code: R

fold here

_____

_____

_____

CENTER FOR CREATIVE LEADERSHIP
PUBLICATION
P.O. Box 26300
Greensboro, NC 27438-6300